Tipperary

by

Desmond O'Grady

Acknowledgements are due to the following publications in which some of these poems first appeared: *The Poetry Ireland Review, Cyphers, Nimbus, The Agni Review, The Old Limerick Journal, The North Dakota Quarterly, The Canadian Journal of Irish Studies, Poetry Canada Review, Guth agus Tuairim, The Irish Press, The Lace Curtain, Horizons, The Limerick Socialist, Krino, Artes (Stockholm), Mediterraneans, Beyond The Shore.*

Some of these poems were published in a limited edition, *Stations*, The American University in Cairo Press, 1976.

House appeared in *Sing Me Creation*, Gallery Press, 1977.

His Ghost to Hamlet appeared in *Poets Aloud Abu*, 1988, for the Poet's Convention, Cork.

The Irish College at Louvain was commissioned by the Minister for Labour of the Irish Government in 1984, Mr. Ruairi Quinn, T.D., to launch the AnCo Training Project at Louvain. The poem was printed as a commemorative pamphlet by the Irish Government's Department of Labour.

Kinsale was written to commemorate the first Kinsale Arts Week, 1988, and printed in that year's programme.

Tipperary appeared in *Bitter Harvest*, an anthology of contemporary Irish verse, selected by John Montague, Scribner's, New York, 1989.

Some of these poems derive from translations I have made, or read, of the poems of other poets.

© Desmond O'Grady, 1991. All Rights Reserved.

Produced with the financial assistance of
The Arts Council (An Comhairle Ealaíon)

Cover painting by John Behan
Typeset & Designed by Johan Hofsteenge
Printed by Colour Books, Dublin
Back cover photograph by John Minihan
Hardback binding by Kenny's Fine Binding, Galway

ISBN 0 948339 78 0 £9.00 Hardcover
ISBN 0 948339 79 9 £6.50 Softcover

Salmon Publishing, The Bridge Mills, Galway, Ireland

for
my friend the painter
Gisèle van Waterschoot van der Gracht

beacons in this temporary archipelago
where we live

George Seferis

Contents

Exordium	11

ORIGINS

An Irish Exile at Liege	15
The Irish College at Louvain	20
The Normans in Ireland	22
Children	25
Circus	26
Recluse	28
Shannon River	30

LIVES

Spring

Sunrise	34
Morning	35
Spring	37
Seabird	38
Woman	39
Farmer	40
Midday	41
Child at Play	42
Works and Days	43
A Son's Birthday	44
House	45
One Easter	46

Summer

Summer Days	50
Fisherman's Family	51
My Green Dream	52
Landlord	53
Midsummer	55
Impromptu	56
Flute Player	57
Pilgrims	58
Wild Dogs	59
Captain Linardos Malamantegna	60
Giséle Triptych	61
Weekend	65
Viola	66

Autumn

Birds of a Feather	68
A Painter on her Birthday	69
Work Break	70
Village Holiday	71
Village Carpenter	72
Funeral	73
Room	74
Asphodels	75
Squall	76
Tell Me No More	77
Breakup	78

Her Window	79
Three Photographs	80
His Ghost To Hamlet	81

Winter

Winter	84
Logbook	86
Hiatus	87
Pub Talk	89
Midwinter	90
Female Visitation	91
Crows of the Imagination	93
Kinsale	94

ENDS

In Memoriam John Tamburro	96
A Drowned Fisherman Aged 21	97
Father	98
A Willow Sprig	103
Hospitality	109
My Rites	113
Graveyard	118
History	119
Tipperary	121

Exordium

I grew up in my medieval Ireland
under her clerical cowl

galvanised in passionless England's
creedless factories

wenched blue Paris
with my green passport

ripened in Roman Italy
on her vineyard culture

sailed the wine-dark Greek sea
among her white archipelago

brooded on Egypt's eyeless Sphinx
between the paws of her mystery

surveyed the southern Russian steppe
from Persia seeking matriarch origins

crossed the godless Atlantic
to plunder America's riches

my return to Ireland
found reclusive haven

dropped anchor berthed
this vessel that's to me

evolved my Ithakian
imagination alone

ORIGINS

An Irish Exile in Liége

Late in the year 845 A.D. - our scholars surmise -
a period of serious Viking stress in Ireland -
   accompanied
by two anonymous companions, one particular
   Irishman

>   Name: Sedulius Scottus
>   Profession: Grammarian Monk
>   Nationality: Hibernian
>   Complexion: Dark
>   Address: Kildare
>   Hair: Black
>   Age: Fortyish
>   Destination: Liége

like so many of his countrymen before and
   after him
took the boat to the Continent, in search of
   stability, peace
and the availability of funds and materials for
   his profession
and livelihood among the illiterate Frankish
   territories hospitable
to the learned. Reading on the journey included
   the *Proverbia Graecorum*.

The north wind made it a rough crossing and
   a harassed arrival.
However, he reached Liége by Christmas to
   Bishop Hartgar's welcome

and appointment as Director of Studies
    at St. Lambert's Cathedral School.
Not surprisingly, we are next told of four other
    Irishmen joining him
but these four probably included his two original
    companions:
        'Charioteers of the Lord.'
        'Lights of the Irish Race.'

Sedulius wrote. Among much else he wrote
    Carolingian poems
in Latin and probably in Irish that, not
    surprisingly, emphasize
his national origin - although nationalism
    was not yet a concept.
He also wrote about exile and, a characteristic
    of exiles, he
makes it quite clear he expects, in fact demands,
    in return for
his 'precious gifts of learning' the best from
    his host the Bishop.
Only the best will help him support the spiritual
    anguish of exile:
        ITEM: One newly constructed burglar-proof
                house.
        ITEM: Interior decoration in the modern
                Continental style.
        ITEM: Refined but functional furniture.
        ITEM: A broad writing table of finest pine.

Sedulius (so named, some opine, after
    that, fashionably
admired in Ireland, Latin poet Caelius Sedulius
    fl. 435 AD
author of the *Paschale Carmen* et al. op.) busied
    himself
not only with writing but with keeping in touch
    with the scholastic
and ecclesiastic centres of Europe and the politics
    of his day.
It is even suggested that he may have visited
    Christian Rome.
He wrote notable commentaries on the eighteen
    volume
Institiones grammaticae of the Mauretanian
    Priscianus
who taught at Constantinople three hundred
    years before.
He also commented on the grammatical works,
    now lost,
of Eutychius Proculus, Athenian 2nd c. A.D.
    Sedulius wrote
on other matters, particularly Paul's Epistles and
    Matthew's Gospel.
His most original work, *De rectoribus
christianis*, concerned
the duties of a prince - written for the son of an
    Emperor no less.
Concerned in part with Church and State
    relations, this work

made an important contribution to the awareness
    and development
of political thought in the Middle Ages. But,
    so like the best,
Sedulius was not beyond borrowing and his
    famous treatise
takes its form from Boethius. Some of his poems
    were written
to both Bishops Hartgar of Liége and Gunther of
    Cologne.
There were poems also to Irmingard, wife of
    Emperor Lothar.
Sedulius knew what he was doing and benefited
    accordingly.

The four points of his world's compass
mark Germany and Africa north and south,
India and Ireland east and west. Rome
naveled his world's Omphalos. Irish churchman
politician that he was, he foresaw the threat
of expansionist ambitions of Moors and
    Norsemen.
He looked cynically on pilgrimages and advised:
if you don't profit from such travel, don't go.

For all his complaint of exile and homesickness
Sedulius cut no mean figure as a social
    personality.
His friends included princes and prelates. He
    held

the confidence of emperors. Pickled with personal
weaknesses, he knew and admitted it openly:
    'My ambition's to die drinking wine . . .
    May God be merciful to this drunk.
    My eyelids droop as I drop into a doze . . .'
Good cuisine, good wine, good talk and all
in the highest company socially and intellectually.
He knew his worth and lets you know it too.
He lived a full life, and if no door was barred
to him it was because he had built his reputation
on solid scholarship and an understanding of human
affairs and frailty. Like most intelligent men, Sedulius,
despite some superficial appearances to the contrary,
was essentially a humble man very aware of his own
insignificance in the universal scheme of things:
    'I read, I write, I teach, I search for truth...
    My heart in shame, laments my sins in life -
    O Christ and Mary, pity this miserable man.'

In all he lived thirteen years at Liége.
He either died and was buried there
or he returned to Ireland. We don't know.
He left the record of his writing of worth
and his public reputation as a learned European.

The Irish College at Louvain

From this, our cloister of the growing mind,
in this historic college where green dreams,
hopes and histories grew before, grow today,
we look down past centuries witnessed Irish
 minds
grow and harvest here perennially. The view
looks much the same as half a century ago -
all of us lived elsewhere then - or three and a half
centuries ago when our forefathers, anonymous
and famous Irish travellers, stopped and stayed
before passing into their futures form our history.

We Irish exile students here today
will always bear in mind our birth elsewhere,
its grim occasions thirty-five decades ago
when poets and priests were hedge-
 schoolmasters
in our Irish fields at home and kept alive
a way of life indelibly our own through
 humanistic
converse. Smuggled abroad, trained at Louvain,
Salamanca, Bobbio and Rome they returned
 home
to train their brothers. Our soul's and our
 society's
salvation remains fraternal effort with whole
 mind.

When we graduate from here to the school of
 hard

knocks on the slopes of our vale of tears, to those
universities of common effort we shall converse
    in,
we may take with us, from the productivity of
    routine,
that geometry which will structure our
    fulfillment
and pass it on to our own when we return home.
The hand of the maker will pass on his cunning,
the mind of the master unravel our precious past
and forge, for the willing young, their adult
    weapons
to confront their futures, shape their personal
    fate.

Upon those plains, in those valleys of our futures
we shall walk and talk through, growing on good
fellowship and fond memories of good
    fellowship;
in that last library of history we shall read in,
that last plain and valley of darkness and light;
in the seed time of our time, on our grave way
    home
to our reward, we may pause, like those historic
    Irish
travellers before us, at the last plain, final valley
and pronounce: as our forefathers passed on all
    they
knew each generation, so do we to you who
    follow us. *Pax tecum.*

The Normans in Ireland

I

Those we read of in books who made history
mesmerize more than the ambiguous story itself.
The rest, in the ebb and flow of Time's mystery,
command as much presence as an empty shelf.

No invasion, before the cruel Cromwellian,
stayed unabsorbed - including that infiltrator
Welsh Patrick and also Strongbow the Welsh
    Norman
armed with the Papal Bull *Laudabiliter*.

Three major foreign movements into Ireland:
Euro-Christian, ethnic Norse, Norman.
Each imported what we lacked first hand:
culture, sea-trade, Christian civilization.

The Christian saved us from the waning Pagan
values of life based on a cattle bargain.
The Norse built harbours, opened the
    Mediterranean.
The Normans changed our tribal law to Roman.

These Normans also centralized our government;
based law and order on the Magna Charta,
the jury, coinage, central Church establishment
and focused life on castle-town trade and barter.

Yet they themselves remained unmaterialistic.
Warlike as Normans, they offered all possible
    peace
to perennially fighting native tribes. The ethnic
Irish absorbed them and adopted their Euro-
    grace.

Where Normans settled Christianity flourished.
They brought religious orders from the
    Continent,
including the Cistercians, eleven forty two A.D.
They brought stability, peace, construction, art.

II

Those names I grew up with at school while
    young,
or work and live with daily now a man,
read etymologically old Irish or old Norman.
The prominent name in my home town was
    Barrington.

These troubadour Barringtons came in the
    eleventh century
with William the Conqueror and brought the
    French *chansons*
de geste of Charlemagne, Arthur and Godfrey.
That love tradition sparked *Noveau Irlande*.

The Limerick Barringtons, all-round Elizabethan,
built and paid for bridges, quay-sides, a hospital
for the poor and patronised both artisan
and artist. They also subsidised the wherewithal

of a *monts de piete*, or poorman's loan-house,
to the wholesome sum of almost twenty six
thousand pounds - the first in the British Isles -
at nominal interest rates to keep up face.

One built Glenstal Castle, the Benedictine
Abbey school today. Another brought
the game of rugby first to these green
fields of Ireland with its sense of sport.

Others grew soldiers, historians, administrators,
politicians, engineers, architects, artisans;
a few fell for the visual arts or for
the Church or Law. One fell to the gun of
    partisans.

In all, for almost a thousand Irish years,
the Barringtons worked to mold a civic face on
their model community for our modern histories.
That's the Norman mind - and European.

Children

Despite that protection a mother
provides for her every child;
despite the fertile powers old women
believe of the blossoming Mayflower,
whitethorn, blackthorn; our children -
beggars of their tomorrows -
will have their day and way,
will all turn cuckoo
and, like the cuckoo,
their hour come round,
they'll jump their fellows,
dump the lot on the jungle,
spread their wings of ambition
and fly off about their
own business crying:
Where? Where?
Seeking! Seeking!

Circus

That's what's left
of all the magic
was our Annual Circus:
that child playing his toy
trumpet, stomping barefoot
on the Fair Green alone.
But to that staccato lyric tempo
of the golden noisy band, now
departed elsewhere, were able
to dance brightly coloured clowns, could
swing trapeze artists, balance human pyramids...

I recall those magic days a man's life ago
when school gave us the afternoon free
and we small, tousled children marched
one side up Madhouse Road to the Circus.
And the mad men and mad women too,
from our local lunatic asylum,
were marched up the shadowed side
with their grey abandoned faces,
their lost or shindig eyes.

And there we crouched in the Big Top - we
the children on one side, they, the lunatics
on their facing other, cry-laughing our lives out,
gasping in terror of a fall; wide-eyed, open-
   mouthed
at the high wire walkers, surefooted as flies.

I remember best that saddest of anonymous
    clowns
blowing his wailing lament on his trumpet while,
unseen by him, his big toe ballooned larger
and larger the more heartfully he blew his lyric
    note.
And then the huge balloon of his toe exploded,
    Bang!
to the delighted shrieks of children and lunatics
    alike.

Recluse

I

From his nextdoor window he watches. She's
   adult
now, deckchaired on her suburban lawn,
fashions and female paraphernalia
scattered about her like playthings; the town -

in the smell of her small car at the front
gate - limp like the moist feathers
of a dead bird found by a boxhedge.
Her one child the same as all others.

The pitch of her voice, precise and precious
as the cutlery sent for her wedding present,
flat on the middle distance enclosing
her semidetatched. Her husband's a pharmacist.

II

Stock still at his window he feels
a suburban's spite in him stirring like lust.
Faced with reflection, he shuffles the slides
of the past with the lightless eye of a ghost.

Settled now, she is one of his more
respectable neighbours. The jargon of mothers
with brand new babies and prams is her forte;
and once a week, for her husband, the
   hairdresser's.

The future, in time, because of the business,
will enlarge the family, the car, the life
insurance and the circle of professional friends.
    Sons
will go to the most proper school there is.

III

He turns away to the correspondence
in the meantime gathered about him like gossip -
dismissing the hate and the urge to explain:
'There's more than gardens and houses between
    us.'

Shannon River

The clouds tricked away my west
coast of Ireland where my Shannon
river fertilises prehistory in our fields,

shadows of those crowded heroes
and horrors of our history, with images
crazed the fantasy of my ancient people.

I joined those shadows, crossed that river
to imagined isles beyond. The river's turned
dream, nightmare. The current continues.
It possesses a fearsome force revitalizes.

LIVES

Spring

Sunrise

Daylight. In gustbags the north wind
rammed all night, as the dolphin shoal
rams death at their single, isolated,
stunned-stupid killer shark.
In the bay's belly grey waves churn,
a tincan of fishguts in a fisherman's fist.
Over the vertebrae of that headland to starboard
sheet lightening splashes, like thrown buckets
of fresh well-water, across the gravelled and
seaweed decks of the sky. Infinity's
    Photographer
narrows the lens of Nature's eye steadily.
The staccato rain on my windowpane
rattles like chains in a convoy dropping anchor.
My room's the navigator's bridge of life's lone
liner ploughs into the storm, the stacked seas
my worst year faced all my years a sailor.

Morning

Sunup sextants my horizon,
fumbles through cloud, as its reflection
off the sea's surface fumbles through
the pewter down-feathers breast
that shearwater. Here I'm a hermitcrab.

The holocaust hammered all night.
Fork lightning, alternate with sheet, flakked
the sky beyond our backhills the open side.
God's acetylene torches hiked to Nature's power.

The cloud's cover breaks. Sun shines through.
The Holy Ghost's rays spoke from their hubcap
   sun,
spike town, sea and land like the silver
and gold holy part high up behind the church's
high altar - the white bird its centre in amber
rich radiance. Miracle stuff! The wind's
dropped, its noise shut up
like a congregation's at consecration.

Hum of a distant fishing boat's engine,
as the organ drone's hum - after the hymn's
ended - continues before the priest's moment.
His wizard words work on his white wafer
as mine now on my white page writing it.

The sea shines calm as a daily communicant.
Our church bell's toll opens this day.
On their dry-stone walls a parish of crows
converse in local cacophony.

Word made flesh,
flesh made word,
my poem's done.

Go in peace
to love and praise.

Spring

Our stony island's hot flower.
Behind, the mountain's riddled
rich hot colour. The wind's
from the south - that signals good
weather. I've dropped the city,
live by the sea in the country.

Halfway through my works and days,
hammered dumb by the town's
torment, I walked out.
Here, in my halfway house,
in my middle years of age,
I start this fresh blank page.

Seabird

Today I am that seabird:
>blackbacked, wheeling
>half high in the sky
>up any cliff's face.

Today I'm that seabird:
>grey breasted, solitary
>at that hour of a good day
>when we'd salute strangers.

Today I am that heron fisher
>plunging salt estuaries
>long before birdtraps
>or slingshots.

Today I'm that gull stands
>on one leg, that flies
>like a lost envelope blown from
>the pocket of our drunk postman.

Today I'm that sea crow
>wings for the heart's headland,
>drops in its glide as the fiddlebow
>drops down its melody playing it.

Today I'm that common small sparrow
>in the focsle of a foreign trader,
>tied up in a white harbour,
>perched by a head of green basil planted
>in a rusty tincan for good luck.

Woman

Since I am thus
since you must matter other,
you thereby may refuse
all makeshift measure.

Since you shape you and you
all this only once,
our this once only,
I wish, I would, I must and shall
state fear and foul
that nothing's other than that one fair child
may pilot the hard hurt heart
home to a harboured honour.

May we,
for crisis' sake,
sail strong
and save some soul,
since we are thus, and thereby fear
all fall.
And may we proud thanksgiving thus
pronounce
for making madness meek.
Amen.

Farmer

He tramps out here daily to his fist-sized fields
through each daybreak's daylight, round our
village road, break whatever weather, spring
or winter. Seventy odd, he reminds me
of my father, who's no farmer - more
my brother who fierce farmer is. We
four free men harness well between us.

Farmer, friend, he makes his day make
sense, as so must manuscript manage I.
His ten green thumbs thumb green throughout
this our rock-broken land lacks water
and he flowers it yearly to its flourishing.

Our mountain bars his far horizon
but he knows our sky's shine and set.
He honours this my book-work much.
I watch him order his day's work
which helps me effort too my daily page.

Midday

The golden sun manages most his day.
Manage too must I. Close by my table
she, housewoman, houseshifts. When able
I scrape out words in lines - mornings.

I reread old stuff my head's forgotten -
forget again. My childhood's nail-bitten
memory muddles matter dumbly. Half
lost I ferreteye her work at kitchencraft.
For agony's solace I scratch that want
within; wait, want again: scrape new start.

Child at Play

In Spring's cautious calm
I watch his every play.

My son, more loved than any loved one,
competes with all in his dare-days'
dodgems. Gifted with power to adapt,
he changes, grows and through childhood's
unbridled wonder, intensely interested
in all life, sees all things fresh and new.

You teach me method how to start my day
as though it were my first or last; example
to praise the power of life in all things.
We do what we can, not what we envision;
then we doubt again what's done.

Each finished effort
merely cuts topsoil.
The what we're after's
somewhere down deeper
in our common clay.

There's a sanity in your
child order I wish for:
four-square proportion.

Works and Days

Here, under this arched porch
the north wind whines, back
of the house, like a traditional
fiddle. Evening: that hour
we water the plants as the sun
dies, glances off the headland,
deepens the gren of our scarce
grass. Terracotta of ploughed fields.

White farm houses, country chapels.
I'm minded of Hesiod. *Works* and *Days*:
rise, bathe, chores. Read. Order
work at words. My lady prepares
our midday meal. Afternoon: physical
labour. Evening: talk. Night: dreams.
Regularity, routine, free imagination.
Peace in works of body, mind, spirit.

My Son's Birthday

This, all your birthday breaks.
The Ides of March sunups
on our houses, wakes us, friends.

Your hour in each our minds
we confront our day's commitments.
Affairs of foreign studs of state
mean zero here to you or us.
We've left all that elsewhere to others,
hold honour of our fellow beyond value.
Grateful for your birth we assure you
we'll not let you down while we're in it,
want that you will carry on what worth
from us you learn, to guide your own.

Today we'll drink and sing
in your strong boyhood's honour.
Forgive us any wrong
we may do in anger.

House

Become men,
their appointed
places found
in their world,
our ancestors
built him, each
one, his house
for his own;
fashioned its entrance
furnished it with
what he'd learned;
fathered a son.

This I do now
in their memory -
and example to you.

Do you likewise
in mine
for your own.

One Easter

All day that downward spiral's
inward silence as she scrubs
clean, tidies her village cottage.
She mumbles to herself all day. Easter
Saturday. Sunday tomorrow. Church.
Prepare the lamb.

Evening. She performs her household
chores mechanically. Traditional houseshift.
Wash those dinner plates. Place the Easter
sweets in the good dishes on the sideboard.
Next: wines, lemonades, liquers, water flasks.
Neighbours visit Easter Sunday. Dye boiled
eggs. Lay the mahogany table: best table
cloth, napkins, cutlery, glasses
from the glasscase. Her trousseau.
Tears swell. Recede.

Her children sleep soundly. Peaceful.
Her fisherman husband, after his hard week's
work, will come home late from the men. She
cleans the lamb for them to roast tomorrow.
Lay out the children's clean clothes, candles.
Her husband's suit and socks hang airing.
Tomorrow he'll wear his shoes, his white shirt
and stroll the village square with his equals.

Almost midnight. The brightly dyed
boiled eggs nestle in the white china
bowl centres her blue kitchen table.
Traditional on Easter Sunday.

She makes sure her little lambs
sleep untroubled in their beds.
With the sweep of habit, she wraps
her shawl about her shoulders. She
puts out her kitchen light. Before
the icons' votive lamp she blesses
herself for each member of her family.
She walks out the door, locks it
behind her. Then she heads uphill.

She strides straight to the cliff's edge
and, with no more hesitation than a blessing,
throws herself into the night and the sea.

Summer

Summer Days

Our days make more sense here this summer
after winter's madness, hurt and loss.
You're here to rest so sleep in late. I
start my morning chores easily, in silence.

After my plunge into this morning's sea
I draw buckets of water from the upper
well that's cleaner, wash the farmer's fresh
fruit and brew our coffee. The sun stronger,
I organise papers indoors on my work table.

Small birds make music under the terrace
eves and acrobat about, or mark a musical
notation on the electricity lines beyond.

Your slow wake up and smile wakes warm
memories. Here we're safe from outside harm.

Fisherman's Family

He sails the smallest serious boat in our harbour;
fathered a fishnet full of fisheyed children.
His wife's a boat's deck of gourd floats, all
humps, hollows; their family team's hooker.
This family lives on top of each other stacked
like fishboxes in one room and a loft bit. He,
regular guzzler of local gutrot though shouldn't.
Angular as anchors, you'd hardly give him, to look at,
his next winter but his fresh flung eyes, smile teeth,
sudden gesture of antagonistic affection, animate.

His grown son's a middlefinger stiffer. Their tiller.
Grin of his father, he's now their night fishing
upkeep, holds their uniqueness. The rest, mere
girls, must get married off somehow, someday.
They're sea gypsies. The smaller fry shoal our village
like sprats. A school to themselves, they swim
    together.
Outsiders to others, they fishtail all weathers no
    matter
their slap fights. A family free of nets entangle us
they net a sure love between them. A sea circus,
    they're
the play within our play - we mere smirker
    courtiers.

They'd never leave a stranger want for sustenance.
Their poverty monuments their pride and
    difference.

My Green Dream

Her soul's splendour breathes from the smiling
   face
of my woman walks over the raw rocks of our
   world
to greet me. My green dream umbrellas her.
   Striding
free there, she's like the black lightening flash of
   ravens
in night flight. Nude, she's reclining clouds on
   the blue
sheet of our sky. She moves in a wind-feathered
intrigue of her own thoughts and that white
   magic,
which laughs from her dark countenance,
   commands
my sphere of sea and sky, mesmerizes a devout
circle about the magic of her passionate presence.

Landlord

Up and at my early morning chores
of household, workroom, I corner eye him
on his bare porch stare hard his void
as though his eyes were eyeless. Not
sea or splendid sun sees he but land -
though stony, by the sea, his own -
with new constructions on it. He
also eyes the fields of others sown
with corn round our bay and silently
spites all that honest labour.

His head's too big for that reptilian body,
bald as the giant turtle and snap beaked
his nose, too. All squat there, he's
neither white nor weather black but dark
and dour, a bulge-eyed toad of calculations.

All round here's the stony land was once
his hard farmed father's. He doesn't work its
surface now but sells off plots to strangers
to build their seaside summer houses. For this
he sits back days to count, recount his makings.
He's my landlord. I'm his tenant can't afford
to buy or build - a mere mote in his visions.

I've never seen him take a swim or wear
a suit. The clothes he's worn look the same
these twenty years. He never buys the paper.
He collects news from others, like the taxman.

He did once work, when this was his father's
    land,
just like other farmers round here; did tend
their goat-herd on the mountain up behind.
Now our sea dingle's in, he's sold his goats
and land and squats and plots from meal to meal.
Some dark strain's devouring him within.

When I'm slow with rent he's darker still
and when I pay, his teeth gnash out his smile.
His colourless, eyeless eyes then glitter.

Midsummer

Today's the strength of the summer's decline.
The sun, castrate, sets on his graveward
course. Endurance and triumph combine
at midday as heaven and hell mouth their Word.

Tonight we'll build our needfire high
with the full flowered oak, kindled east
and west on our mucklewheel. The old way
used a gallow's rope. That day's past.

In the bonfire's blaze we'll eat roast meat
and drink, dance frantic round the flame.
Before the dawn we'll bear fire's light
by stick or candle safely home

and ring our bells loud: 'John! St. John!'
That's a practice long dead now in town.

Impromptu

My love's seagull dips through your dark eyes,
My dreams cataract your wild hair
White pigeon thoughts break in your laughter
And the man worth your soul lives nowhere.

The wave's top tumbles your breastbone,
Royal sailing ships rock in your heart
Your wide shuttled net's imagination
Trawls shoals in my fathoms of want.

A dark chapel's architect round you
Your face forms an icon not known
No priest yet has prayed on your altar
But this sea flies one broken-winged crow.

Flute Player

Nose ridged butty man
he fingers his song's flute
to pursed lips. Pauses. Then,
head thrown back to pitch it,
closed eyes face to the sky,
he gives us his sound
for the processional. High
his held note, supple his bend
of the song's grace. We lads
and girls sing with gladness
behind him dancing while he leads
the lengthening line of his chorus
to festival round the narrow streets
of our village all holding hands.

Pilgrims

Trudged all day
through brazen sun. That
endless track stony
as any new testament's.
Our perspiration salty,
our horizons misted
through eyebrow's sweat.
All the wells brackish,
the air acrid. We neophytes
slogged on, relentless.
We stopped once at some
stony farmhouse. An old
toothless woman eyed us.
No man. A fool-child woman
also in the gable's shade. We
wanted water. We drank,
thanked, shoved on. When
we got to the place sought
it wasn't there. Perhaps
the signs were wrong.
So we turned around, again
trudged back in blazing sun
past dry wells, abandoned
threshing circles cracking.
We found what we sought
at home....

Wild Dogs

Our dogs round here
thrive savage. Mongrel mangy,
they gang in groups
like gangsters.
They're barred in town.
There they'd beat them blind
or kill them off at night.
Conger-faced, their snouts
whole ferrets, they fang ferocious.
Provoked, they'd rip off half
your calf in a snarled flash;
tear out the throat of your purebred.
They guzzle garbage, butcher's offal.
The bitches bite first and worst.
Their eyes' cast would galvanise tincan.

Captain Linardos Malamantegna
1916-1988

Ashore, he stalks his home's harbour.
Anchored, his ship's hulk huddles her mooring
wharf. All focsle, he struts his bowsprit
forehead two thirds through our mid noonday
dock-bar talk, tamer of our sea's cavalry.
Two generations into his rich age he's a sail
full of old guff, cracked stories, advice-talk
on anywhere whatsoever. He's our Captain.

Hospitable his household, noble his lady -
eyes fixed on her home port's horizon line.
And I've seen him, returned, sail
that bowsprit through their bedroom
balcony overlooks our harbour, walk
in straight off it all soft sea-swear.

I eye him sometimes talk childlike to pup
grandchildren, croak old songs in their ears.
Fiercefaced as fury, his glass-lift lifts lighter
than a gull's wing in fair weather while his voice
sounds the chain of his anchor's drop. Friend-men,
we sail sometimes together to elsewhere and back.
Sea nights he sleeps, the tiller rope wrapped round
his shoulders for warning to wake him should we
hit wave weather. Where else sails his like now?

Sail safe.

Gisèle Triptych
'colours are the joys and pains of light'
- Goethe

I

Here on Paros island of the malleable marble
    Phidias worked, where wine-
stricken Archilochus - cricket of iambic satire,
    elegiacs, worshipper
of Demeter our corn goddess, killed by Callondes
    the Crow, of Naxos,
in a bar brawl - you m'lady, and I, separated by
    our Taishan Mount Vigla,
our lookout of individuality, lookout our
    seperate imaginations' windows
on our common sea's dingle of mutual manners
    and *meltemi* storms and stories.

Thoughts of the forces pushed us here in the first
    place: idealists roaming
the Greco-Roman world seeking a place to settle,
    finally settled for here.
Now, unrelated widow and widower, both alone
    with our separate endeavour,
you this year slammed into seventy; aristocratic
    profile to the wave, strong
as that first day I remarked you stride through
    Naoussa harbour twenty
years ago. For all the change by process, success
    or failure, life, death,

what's valuable cannot change but contracts to a
    focused still centre
of certainty. To continue to do, make, stimulate
    mind and spirit
'this is not vanity' and to maintain the memory of
    friendships; the tribe
made through the doing, costs, claims no quarter
    but delights.

II

Day dawns when love's no more the pressure of
    passion but maturely
cultivates into the confidence of companionship
    enhances commitment
of passion in all endeavour. Lone purgatorial
    years learning. For you
the condition of fear that reigned through two
    wars in our times
followed by 'small war upon small war' passed
    unspoken. People forbore
its mention, praying culture would detonate the
    explosive safely.
You hid friends from anarchic Nazi thugs.
    Courageous statement.
Wars may funereal down to local battles,
    skirmishes at home,
but we both work grateful for the light can shine
    in obscurity.

Darkness wreaks destruction; death of
   imagination, spirit, though all
ease into individual darkness - preferably with
   song, the dance,
images of tragic laughter, constructs of tribal
   memory - and leave our record.

It seems there occurs hiatus in our middle years
   of making
we must battle then. Afterwards, the power
   that's life in age,
that clarity of experience, vision, drives against
   all disillusion.
We start anew. This marks the moment when we
   get back to basics,
ellipse to Euclid's axioms: sphere, triangle,
   square, rectangle, cone.

III

Events, public, private or personal, complete
   their cycles
and the exhausting life of creation shall start
   again. Events
outside our personal control like war,
   harassment, effort,
(that force or urge us to another place, state of
   mind, beginning)
vitamin renewal; provoke a progress, a power
   previously ungenerated.

Curiosity and change compel the *kunst* of form,
    charge its action. I
only record passing thoughts of passing times.
    Process! The artist
you, brings to mind Eleusis' Persephone,
    pomegranate bud in hand;
and me, at this your table, sings through that
    Orphic harper found in our
Kyklades. Wise Simonides of Ceos said
    'painting's poetry's silent song;
poetry's painting that sings.' That Koré's plaited
    braids you know well
reflect for me the years our lives plaited too, and
    you've waxed
nothing less than gracious kind to me and mine,
    tough times together.

Weekend

Remember that rise and fall against the cliff
of the lighthouse beacon beyond the bunched
monastery? The sky stretched dark except where
the sun's last flush descends to a limped spark.

We saw our archipelago of safe islands
within sure sight, sure reach of each other,
hospitable harbours within hail of small boats;
promontories like articulated limbs of statues
gesticulating from the niches of their pantheon.

The sun set, we descended tumuli of stones
with laughter in contentment's surrender.
Our poor, innocent adventures of those days
never again knew more inexpressible moments.
That joyous cry of liberty bombolates outwards
multiplying itself to new horizons. Remember?
We descended to hospitable huddles of light
as yet unaware that decay, destruction, lay
off shore; pirates in full sail for our hearts.

Viola

In those crystal globes of hidden tears at dusk,
tears that drop unseen within from the thorns
of passion's sacrificial crown, your physical
presence rearouses unspoken recollections of
    past
beauty and the brackish bitterness that created.
And this confuses me all over again, torments.

Your radiant eyes reflect the shooting stars of our
    sky
and the long nights of our nearby fishing port
    after sunset,
like the beaded ivory necklace of desire round
    your throat,
or your proffered bouquet of asphodel this
    evening that now
decorates the battlefield of my room with your
    absence.

Your statuesque stride opens a new mountain
    road
through my dusk and paces these words I can't
    tempo.
So, silently, I beg you to my mountain madness
by the light of our common lantern to illumine
    my dusk.

Autumn

Birds of a Feather

They wing in each evening, close
across the bay from the open sea
when the moon's up. They're a love pair.
One leads, the other follows and they call
each to each in their flight - a love call
that directs. Alone here at my word-sorting
I await their cry nightly for its lyric
reassurance. It gives me pause and stirs
strong thoughts of you now flown elsewhere.

Landed, they step about the beach beside
the sea's seamed edge like courtiers in their
palace of rock, wrack and sea sound.
When they're late I'm nervous, fuss-fiddle
with distractions. Their first cry heard
I settle back and steady. It's their hour
and I feel surer, knowing now they're here,
as word arrived of you brings you here.

Some mornings I creep up to watch them.
Their stilt legs, thin and grained as twigs,
knob at the knees; their haughty heads held high;
tapered bill bent at the tip.
Shapely feathered frame majestic,
their elegant reserve teaches.

This morning I walked round the bay.
Suddenly, in the rushes, I found the cock
dead. The female's flown away.

A Painter on Her Birthday

Another autumn cuts the air. Our clear
sea round us cools. The colours of
our archipelago turn heraldic.
All others gone, we settle back
to daily forge our separate lives.

You, in your retreat, recede for days
to paint. I hold my hours in stringed
words of imagined things, like beads.
This turns our season of the year
before the silence of dead winter.

This year to celebrate your birthday
I applaud your high achievements. War
years hiding friends at home from satanic
strife; the living work in word and paint
fashioned despite darkness; friendship's fortress
architected through strength and loving's loss.

Evening settles. Our glad day declines.
The goat herd's homing bells our sunset.
Autumn ripens in our bay's sparce fields.
A lone crow caws westward down the inlet.
The shoreline's shuffled boulders bundle
for their night, as friends do elsewhere.

This twilight's ours. All trouble
from our pasts still seeks solution.
Your Muse's mandolin will conjure some.

Work Break

Autumn. I stroll the summer deserted
shore. The sea's paw fumbles shells
in nature's change-till like shekels.

Insecure, pickled from habit,
I collect sea urchins.

Nature's silent side,
manifest to us, lives and dies
blind to its daily monstrous glories;
accomplishes zero. Our burden
that. Functional, we may take -
despite our tendency to self-destruct.

Inside, my baffled brain
corrodes; holed as limerock,
pitted as sand with rain,
ravelled as seawrack.

I saw a cow calve
in that field once.
The afterbirth swung in wind.
She tongued the calf warm.

Afterwards, I shared a bottle
in his house with the farmer.
'Life,' drank he. 'Life,'
my mumbled antiphon.

Village Holiday

Holiday today, all day. We taste the new-made
wine. The farmers, in from around for morning
Church, gather about in clots; stiff in sweaty suits
and boots, chins razored sharp as scythes;
hatchet faces hatched as their ploughed fields
they'll start tomorrow. Our greybeard, local
    stump
of a parish priest's in the thick of them. Outside,
the donkeys, tethered in knots, attend like
    drovers.

Today's all smile and handshake, toast and drink
long life. Teeth flash smiles at a yarn. Glint
of an old man's still young mischievous eye.
Some deals get made: rent a plot for ploughing;
arrange that bull for service; agree on next year's
prices; discuss a match, a dowry; this day last
    year;
who died since then; dread of a too cold winter.
Rude fingers, rough as drystone walls, clutch
glasses gently for each toast to next year.

The women, hidden in their houses, make small
    talk
on illness, marriages, dowry houses, childbirth.

The young, in pairs, tonight
will dance to local music.
That's our way round here.

Village Carpenter

His mouth's shut tight as a coffin's lid.
That burglar underlip juts out like a lever
or handle. His eyes' cast's fixed
as casket knobs. He doesn't talk.

Relentless tomblike silence marks
each his every workway's come and go.
No rumpus ruffles his rhythm. Never
short of work, his future's fast.
He's the card carpents our coffins.

I've never caught him laze or drink
with any others. He's the loner always there;
sticks out as our only worker here wears a black
apron. Funereal his lope-walk about business.

In early years he cracked no smile
nor glanced to notice when I'd pass
daily, frequently - he there in his dark
box workshop about his mystery matters
with his rule measure, chisel and mallet.

Those years, young, I worked surely;
saw much to make, accomplish, master.
His shadow cast no darkness on my mind
nor registered his gloom intention. The other
day I sat idle, drinking whiskey. He loped
past. He smiled - his bared gold teeth brassy
as an engraved coffin's plaque. One to one,
we now salute each other every day.

Funeral

His heart hit this morning
unloading his truck. Gone by noon,
he's all our town's talk. Some
reckoned him the richest round bar none.

He made his money making
that stuff we all drink daily.
Didn't touch it himself - wisely.

Tank thick, waddle walk
he gave his sons agoran grace
had nothing noticeable
to do with himself, head on.

His face faced heaven, his wallet pocket
hell from his open coffin as we men
lugged him round our village
for his last good look and luck. Then
up our Stony Batter to our Stony Joke.
There we dropped him down for good.

Later we talked his worth -
partly as man, partly as money
partly as good old sort
while we drank his gutrot stuff.

Room

On the wall of this room
hangs a common picture:
a sailboat sailing dark
seas into a shadowed sun
neither risen nor set.

It reminds me of childhood
when I'd go down to gaze
at the rare ship that sometimes
sailed into that abandoned port
up north where I'm from. There
I daily dreamt of far off cities
white and clustered like crystals
in bright sunlight by blue seas
fringed by waving palms, flowers.
I planned to sail there one day.

Here, in this harbour, among
this huddle of fishermen's cottages
waving palms, on this blue sea,
at times, I remember, long for,
that abandoned port up north.

Asphodels

Asphodels of images
this morning fly in and out
of my room like swallows
and meander my mind.
The sun shafts light
through the venetian shutters
and, between the pauses
of these lines, occasionally
I glimpse a black bird
fly off outside like an image
of you out of reach.

Squall

Suddenly, a squall between us.
Emotions rattle, scatter like pages
on my table in a wind gust.

My calm catatonicised, I storm out.

From our window you shout love.

Rage blown out round the house
I return becalmed. For a while
we sail fair weather.

Tell Me No More

You say you want
another way, away.
Love, tell me no more.
I don't want to know.

You brightened my vision
my years of chosen blindness.
Those years, crablike,
I baulked sidewards.

I believed the pen
never deserts her cob,
remain deceived.

Love, tell me no more.
Youth, like the moping moth
burns out in the flame
of worldwise fire
and the distraction's merely
that breeze may tremble the flame
but never extinguishes it.

Breakup

Fishermen give back to the sea
as they take from it,
leave old boats to the wreckage
of the waves that sailed them.

Far from you now,
on a deserted beach
I saw two ships'
skeletons in the sand
and a corroded anchor.

I stood reminded
of the two of us
our last winter together,
of the sea's severity,
of sightless rudders,
lost anchors, timbers
breaking up.

Her Window

This evening,
boats back,
I passed her window
her last summer here.

That hour, when
the sun sets
on my mountain, we
all stroll our village.

Passing,
I glanced sideways,
pronounced her foreign
name. The window's
still there. She's gone.

The sun burns
the bay, my blood.
Darkness cowls
the sun, cauls
my mind.

Our crowd's
still here;
live's our same
village routine.
Some, married;
have children.
Some, older,
died.

Three Photographs

That sun sinks again, shines
through the ruins remain round me
self-exiled here. I stare at that,
my stolen photograph of you
aged eight. You stare
back at me. I stole it
for your child's smile
I fell for later when first
we met and willed would mother me my son.

Beside it I've propped a photo of our son and me.
He and I gaze, as in *bas-relief*, across at adult
you in my third snapshot. We looked marked
   men.
I fear for fated children. We stare you, marked
   too
forty odd years later. But your child's look's
gone now from your adult face and eyes.
Our past's dead. Our present abides.

His Ghost to Hamlet

Now we face off alone
Prince, we may talk
man to man; now you ascend
these tortuous stairs of your youth
and feel you stand existential as an ant
in this adult antiworld of institutions.

I have never thought of your glad glance
to me, Prince, without my own glad glance back.
For now, yours looks like a bird's nest fallen
in Fall. Defenceless as youthful indirection.
Reality, confronted, presents precisely this,
   Prince.
Your helpless hands fall apart; your new crown,
your sacred sword feel too big, weigh too heavy
and your princely feet feel feckless in your
   knight's
new boots. Now you must ride into the solitary
tournament of it without having jousted at all -
   yet.

That's the only life I have some acquaintance
   with.
Expect no applause, no speeches, no firework
   celebrations;
only masks, Prince, masks. And manipulating
   manoeuvres. All
interests secret their rehearsed styles of insidious
   sincerity.
Therefore a father must sometimes take his Prince

firmly by the neck and shake him, somewhat.

A prince must decide for life, or lose, Prince.
We may believe in the crystalline chiméras of our
imagination but must confront the bodies
    corporate,
learn to breathe in the bureaucracies of
    advancement.

You will know peace, Prince. Meanwhile
accomplish what you may. That's peace.
The rest's not silence but remains eternal
with me, your ghost. Renege what's easy:
ephemeral elegance, elasticity. A prince
must stand decisive and assertive. Always.
With princely patience, learn eternal watching.
Accommodate yourself to your straight-backed
chair, to your crystal ball, and keep your cold
eye on that ant hill and on that clock.

Good night, Prince. There's to get done:
reorganise economies, draft new decrees,
decree new dreams, legislate new liberties.
Tonight you're present beside me under our stars.
What you may make may never make for
    memory
but remember that to make records better
than not to make at all, Prince.

Goodnight! Sweet Prince!

Winter

Winter

Day dawns on this my winter's Ireland.
November's the month rounds off our Celtic year
sacred to those dear souls no longer here
but in multiple ways brought back to mind.
Behind my black barred gate I settle in
to work my winter until spring return.

Beyond that dry stone wall this dawning day
among those dying elms, evergreen yews
of our graveyard here, that murder of resident
    crows
rattle black feathers, scuffle their black nests,
    caw.
Here's my home-harbour and my final rest-place.
In shape of a camel a cloud graves my distance.

Our personal watchdog eye in the unmapped sky
keeps sleepless watch on when we stop, when
    go.
Should it once blink then we - as we well know
happened to others - get wrecked, go lost, may
    die.
Faith in our mythic powers of intuition
will find us our appointed, final destination.

The women loved we icon in our time.
Lost companions turn shadows in our twilight.
Deeds done and sung, forgotten out of sight
in attics of memory, revived, sing out of tune.

The only legacy we may pass from or on
is lone example and what's left not done.

Some primitive plumbline steadies within my
    head.
I'm back now safely where I once left from
for fortune. I find my only son has flown
on his own course of conquest through the mud
of his world. Anchored, I'm settled down
again in origins. I've claimed, restore, my home.

When my last day will fail to dawn for me
they'll walk me over the way outside this
    window
and plant me in our graveyard under that crow
perched on that dying elm in my marked
    rockery.
Down at our local hostelry they'll drink my
    health
and harm; drink more; then talk my times and
    worth.

Logbook

My morning's work-hours done
I meander round our broad bay's
bend before it's lunchtime as though
I'll find you paddling as usual under
our friend's white stone house -
bowed head thinking your thoughts
as though looking for shells, pebbles.
But you've gone absent elsewhere.

Winter's on me. I work now here alone.
Cove after baptismal font cove I come
on no person's human footprint in
the sea's washed sand and shingle.

Except for the crow's crude caw, jingled
goatbells, our mountain's mute. Our friends'
house locked up, I sit silent and seek
your form in the wind-shaped volcanic
boulders ring the indifferent sea's edge.
I try not to make my madness madder.

Hiatus

I. Blank

My blue sky clouds out today.
Rough seas roll around our bay.
Our face to faces too look grey.
Her quarry gangs my head.

We may not always hope for sun.
Our royal moments rarely come.
At hours as this what must be done
says beat out lines like lead.

II. Plan

Alone in this cloister I plan
my possible future.

My poems record my past
or passing. What's ahead

skulks out of sight tomorrow.
Art's from excitement. Must excite.

III. Winter

This morning's mine.
All's equipment.
My father, in the shade
that's his year's cloister,
reads. Nothing registers.

Surrounded by my books
my mind's muddled.
I understand everything,
remember nothing. Each
day's light disintegrates.

IV. You

Through my morning
window swifts fly
like musical notation.
They orchestrate my day.

In the pause of each
phrase's pause I glimpse
black wings swift
across my vision.

An image of you
across our day.

Pub Talk

Here, in these safer reaches of my Irish harbour's
mad winter, I look across the breakers on my
   Atlantic.
Alone, I'm more like those medieval Munster
   monks
hived here before in the last millennium. Talks
with solitary fishermen in our crowded pub echo
that vintage. 'The wind and tide ride high.
Relax and drink. We'll sail no boats today.'
As if to say: 'Who shall we tell of our secret
   thinking.'
A kind of solution to our silence was the Viking.

Midwinter

Dull memory of light...
Struggle for sustenance
against weakness.

Rain. Fog.
I suffocate, choke
blind images.

Scattered paraphernalia
of summer's abundance left
in a midwinter garden:
shambles of broken
chairs, crates, warped
tables, maimed trellis,
rusty iron, tubers,
brambles gone berserk.

Female Visitation

I

Darling mantis of my mind -
the others called you Flower,
I don't know why - this evening
after our sun set,
in the almost dark,
you stood here again
beside me - poised, long-jawed,
with that devastating outbreak
of your bared laughing teeth.

Upright over me,
you darkly devoured
my personal twilight.

II

Words, Words
old mole,
winged
on woman wizardry.
Buzz, buzz
old truepenny,
you brazen
belladonna you...
all thunderstorm
no sunset.
I don't believe you.

You left so suddenly
with such short
soliloquy. Surely
you still had lips
to say your say?
I won't trust you again.

Crows of the Imagination

Bearing mythologies on their macabre flight
they pass at nightfall with their steady wingbeat
and the glorious dead hear the scrapings of scribes
record their ominous activities for posterity. They're
headed for their makeshift nests in old rookeries
and the clatter of their awkward wings shatters my
  sunset.
They overfly historical battlefields and stop to strut
on their splayed talons among the lopsided
  headstones
of our graveyards at evensong with those black
  sparks
from their rattle of stiff feathers. Sometimes,
  you may
see crows reflected in the eye's glance of a marked
child - a child chosen to tombstone a fixed place
in the tradition. Crows may easily confuse the
  giddy
weather-cocks of angels in that manic monotony of
  their
flight and pause for the company of gargoyles on
  cathedrals
for gargoyle converse about the curlicued rose-
  windows
of angelic imagination and later fly through the gaze
that's the moon's sacred observance or our vigil.
Finally, crows descend on the slumped shoulders of
  we,
embattled, committed, at day's end; then cáw
  triumphant.

Kinsale

Cúin tSaile or *Ceann tSaile*:
Quiet of the Sea or Head of the Ocean.
Either way, home-haven. Here we all
live 'blow-ins': exiles, or exiles from
exile. And we 'love our ease, our idleness.'
You would too if you lived here among us.

The Bandon river finds sea exit here,
Atlantic spawning salmon entrance.
Kinsale origins flowered beyond the Ice sphere
which makes of Time and History a nonsense.
Here Celtic alternative order fought, died,
sixteen one; left us Ireland's modern divide.

We sleep side by side, together,
enjoying harmony's just measure
without weapons on display for war.

ENDS

In Memoriam John Tamburro
d. 1977

Today they drink their funeral wake wine
in desolate silence at their bare cafés
throughout the ancient towns of Italy. Giovanni
Tamburro is dead. Today their eyes fix
on the blank distance of others' emigrations.
Today the pietás of the country parishes
rock back and forth in their plain chant
of grief. *Oremus.* Giovanni Tamburro
lies dead in far away America.
The bells of their campanile toll his hour.
No funeral for him in unknown Sette Frate
with horse, hearse and cassock. He's stretched
dressed up in an Italo-American Funeral Parlor.
He left forever, a gentle young man
with one battered suitcase to sweat
for the earned dollar of the poorman's labour.
He married his own kind, gave the world
a big son and beautiful daughter. *Grazia Dio.*
At the time of his death the Pope in Rome
spoke out against Communist crises in Europe:
Ave Kaiser Viva il Duce Viva il Papa
That's their history: Romans, Italians, Romans.

Ave Atque Vale

A Drowned Fisherman Aged 21
David Berry, d. 1980

    He rolls on his rocky crevice
    in the twilit fathoms of Ocean.

My writing hand gropes blindly in the swell
to close his young man's eyes with verses.
He has put his youthful anxieties, ambitions
to rest forever. His winding sheet's a wave,
his graveyard the Atlantic Ocean.

His white bones sparkle as sun on sea, his coffin-
clasps God's seashells. Anemone scribble his
   epitaph.

Wheeling gulls wail for him. The winds
   whispers His service.
His eyelids locked closed on his seabed, he
   dreams
of the drowned of armadas, populous as
   plankton.

    He rests on his rocky crevice at peace.
    We rock in our fathoms of loss.

        Óchone!

Father
d. 1981

I

The bush telegraph works. Your news
with its urgency came by boatman to my
here remoteness via people you'll never meet
in this foreign to you country. I dropped
everything at once and made it, in time,
twenty-four hours later, thanks to friends.

This hour comes to all, once: Father dying
come home. You didn't think I'd make it. Home
now I find you low but stubborn. Life. Death.
The meandering mind of old age. And yet,
that old humourosity still. To go out on an aside.
Should we let you slip out in your own bemused
    time
or force your flight? Go in peace, not in pain?
Aware, not comatose? Has man a right, some
responsibility, to help man go? This, my
    solitary's
return road to origins and originator saddens.

II

Finding you there on that alien hospital bed
asleep with your false teeth half slipped out
of your sagged mouth. Your skin a fine
linen stretched tight over your skull

reminding me of the skulls found in old
abandoned graveyards as an adventure hunting
boy. This is the beginning of your end I've not
wanted to think about face on but now must
face. What may we say to our dying fathers,
    expect
our sons to say to us dying? Later, outside in
    sun,
we sons discuss the practicalities of your going:
coffin, grave, tombstone, distribution of
    possessions;
also if, when my day comes, they're to bring me
home or put me down where I fall, abroad.

III

That alien hospital awaits. I'm afraid. Not
of the operation but of the loneliness of wards
I've known visiting hospitalized friends - ailing,
dying. In hospital there's a sterility in that
    machine
of method and manners frustrates the giddy
imagination. And those gaunt faces staring,
bed after bed, ward after ward, as in
    concentration
camps, staring. It's a compound of loneliness
visitors feel loathe to stay long in - hardly
arrived thinking of leaving. Except, perhaps,
    women.

They sit, as in church, in their resigned patience,
or lie like taking a late morning in bed at home,
or as though in old fashioned confinement at
   home.

My only personal hospital time I was seven after
that accident the night before my First
   Communion.
Was there an omen in that fall? So many falls
   since.
No hospital for those but time, endurance. No
plastic surgery of the spirit for those scars.

IV

You've pulled through again, at least
physically for now and, though your meandering
mind wanders more and worse, you're out
of that concentration ward and in a happy
Home. We only feared your wandering
out on the road like one of the children
and getting bashed into eternity as my son's
   other
grandfather did, walking home to his Italian
   village
from American Boston. At least you're home,
yet might get the notion to go back again
to your birthplace too on foot, or cheat
and try to drive your car there. Disaster that.

The pity of the stubborn mind dying cell
by solitary cell; the stubborn rowing
with married children; irritation
with growing grandchildren who cannot
understand. King Lear's old gaga story. He
wandered off too but had a faithful
caring Fool to talk to, watch for accidents.
Not you, too reserved always to make close
friends or suffer fools gladly. The solitary aged
are seldom beautiful to behold - those vacant
eyes, peeling hands, sagged jaw or tight mouth.
Only in the fresh transparency of death
does a youthful freshness return, ironically.
Is recovery more desirable than painless release?

V

After blessed respite you rallied. I returned
to finish a task undertaken long before
    elsewhere,
America, a place you'd never witnessed although
I'd promised you once, in a shaded carriage
beside the Pyramids, we'd take that trip together -
you game with widower's gaiety to gallant
anywhere those halcyon days. I'd hoped
you'd hold on long and strong enough
to help me hold high my Harvard trophy,
savour tribal triumph as you savoured all
extramural experience with your specially
feint smile of satisfaction, *coup d'oeil*.

Their phone call cancelled that. 'He may not
last the night. Come home.' I grabbed my son,
flew. Sons big enough must carry their
    grandfather's
coffin beside their father and family men.
    Tradition.
        Our women see us out.
        Our men see us under.
Arrived, we proudly buried you beside your
    bride.
Then by God you were gone! May God take
    your side.
Slán.

A Willow Sprig
- for Professor John V. Kelleher at The Charles River
on the occasion of his retirement from Harvard, 1986

Now 'that Aprille with hise shoures sote'
transforms this, our Ireland's Spring morning,
I write, alive and well, from my after life here;
    not far
from your people's Clondrohid, on Cork's Kerry
    border.
There I, a summers' child in Coolea, Ballyvourney,
    learned
that Irish which brought us together later; master,
    pupil.
I've not been back there since, for wandering the
    world, but
surely we'll share all that soon, now you've retired
to your after time. 'Better a patch than a hole'
the Breton proverb says. Time gapes its gap, my
    friend.

In this Kinsale of lost Irish hope, 1601,
I daily wrestle to winkle back into that self
within myself, before I curled my world's whorl
where I fortuned to find you, winkled in Harvard's
    Widener.
I wrestle, too, to keep this wolf inside the door,
not the reverse. The crows caw cruel example:
'first up mornings, first to bed at night.'

We met one short genealogical generation ago
on your shore our common Ocean: me bearing this

my personal beehive cell of madness to your
   monastic
door in that modern monastery that's walled
   Harvard.
Another resident Alien then in my America's
   Athens, I saw
myself nothing more or less than translated
   European Irish
and stood outside Widener 17 recommended by
   your chemist
Limerick friend gave you young hospitality, a
   travelling
scholar, this side. He finally saw you that, your side.
   Your
hospitality received, accepted me, given neophyte I
   appeared,
and gifted me my mortal reality; your form of
   fosterage -
giving of heart and head. Me awkward in your cell
   there;
'too green for firewood, too wet for kindling' - yet!
That democratic opportunity exampled this Celt's
   wander,
compass and sextant of navigation. Spring months
   thereafter
you walked and talked me your Charles River
   banks
(as Uncle Feathereye walked me a child my
   Shannon)

mythologising. Comradeship! You reminisced
 your father's time
when Irish-American workers walked from
 Lawrence to labour
building Boston, then walked back home,
 weekends. America!
'Dig deep, throw high, the pay's the same.'
 England's Irish.
Walking the thawing Charles, I couldn't say much
 back. I listened,
learned, then wrote my muddle down on paper
 later, brother.
So many singing friends have since free-sailed down
 the River.
'Some here, more no more, more again lost alla
 stranger.'

All said and done, then, I said what I should do after
 and did
and left you grateful eulogy will outlive us both,
 they say.
Since then I've done for others what thou didst for
 me. Tradition!
I returned once (older, wiser) to finish off what we'd
 begun. You
graciously encouraged yet again - lefty, lefty. Then
 'twas done.
The 'test of the bow' at that age. Process appears
 more appreciation,

less understanding, of 'the reality of experience'
    through works
and days and books; memory's more mutable than
    the Muse.
'Read everything,' you advised at parting. 'Build a
    broad base.'

All those years you spent your days
making order of our Irish genealogies,
sense of our Annals,
giving us identities:
people, places, paraphernalia...

Not to talk of your ordering
the thoughts, talk and theses of others.
All your books
written by others.

Diminuendo in our days
does not deter direction.
Awareness is all.
Then curiosity,
and its record.

A life lived.
A record left.

I urge you now: do not retreat among those
    reclusive shades

on upper corridors or buried in basements behind
   old tomes.

Cross the sea again for the island homes of
   imagination
and make your circuit here, as once you did,
   aspirant.

Here you'll find my retreat,
an exile from exile, easily,
by word of mouth.
Bealoideas.

My retreat overlooks two headlands, one sea.
All year long my gate's flung open wide,
my turf fire lit.
No plans but poking in books
and pushing slow lines of verse across the page.
And for daily punctuation
slow strolls through trees by the sea
along the Low Road to The Spaniard Pub.
There, serious talk over porter of this world's
   charted courses
with retired seamen of Scilly Village and their
   fishermen sons.
(They hold mighty views on all muckle matter).
And, in these long evenings, good music;
the sound held in half light after the instrument's
   played it.

Or reading poems aloud to each other.
A man must 'live out his three bushes.'

Make a home.
Father an heir.
Write a book.

Now with the long summer days that stretch into it,
young men out bouling country byways
to shouts of fellow encouragement,
I'll watch for you on the Low Road
walking to meet me.

In that ancient way of manners
I send this sprig of willow across that moat
of our common Atlantic to you
thinking....

Note: *Willow Sprig*: It was an ancient Chinese custom to give a sprig of willow to a departing traveller.

Hospitality
to *Donna Marcella Altieri, January 1991*

This January in Rome you face the final decade
of our second Christian millenium. Your side
of your multifarious, magnanimous family and we
friends attend you in your home as queen bee
who bestows the honey of human kindness about
as the finest kind of pure-bred European aristocrat.
For me, you radiate one of the few I've known in
    this selfish
world who gives without a thought for gratitude,
    without a wish

for yourself but friendship's sterling love. Your
    seclusion
relishes nothing more than the presence of family,
    grandchildren
and friends in frivolous repartee or serious
    discussions
of giddy girlhood or the time's events of family or
    nations.
Your spontaneous and continuous gift to me is the
    hospitality
of your family home, your sisterly heart, your very
    country.
And that at a time when the structures of my
    personal life
collapsed at the cost of my family tenure,
    my very motive

for being and I was forced to swallow my dreams
   like a sword-
swallower in the circus, suffer my soul's purgatorial
   period
alone. The intuitive invitation of your hospitality
   gave me
the chance of distance from that nightmare and
   age's timely
space and silence to evaluate what of myself is
   salvageable.
Today, for your birthday, I thank you in the only
   honourable
way I know how to handle and hope our Roman
   times together
have released some relief from your concerns as
   mother and grandmother.

Your mode of life is what I've long aspired to,
   worked to live:
peaceful days in this rich country with life's brief
   time to give
to personal pursuits - books and writing, music and
   friendship
and in the evenings the indulgent revery of
   memory's gossip.
Then, when occasion warrants, visits to cultural
   events
and like-minded friends in Rome dear to us both
   and our wonts.

The wealth of the spirit is evaluated in such
 currency of kind.
And there's no greater peace found than in the
 creative habit of mind.

You've richly lived the lives of four generations in
 full
and sometimes frivolity. I laggard one behind you
 still
since my grandchildren don't know me yet. I hope
 one day
both yours and mine will meet and share their
 personal way
of life as happily as we do ours and pass it on to
 theirs.
By then let's hope our world's powers will wage no
 wars
as they seem intent to do this week of your peaceful
 birthday.
Why should our children beget their own to go to
 war to kill and die?

Dear heart Marcella, your family and friends today
 gladly
indulge you, each in their personal way that
 celebrates your worldly
advent. I'm honoured to stand your adopted friend
 among them.
Whatever good or ill may befall either of us before
 the millenium

locks, I pray that we and ours sleep sound,
 protected from life's harms.
The natural love you unselfishly, inimitably bestow,
 returns;
reflects from those you've bred and reared, from
 each friend.
Whatever the nature of our times, the love's all that
 matters in the end.

My Rites

That day comes in common lives
when we arrange our last affairs
while we have health and time. It grieves
   many to so confront arrears
in rent or mortgage: What goes to whom?
Whether an urn, a headstone or tomb?

Back from my daily musing stroll
among the plots across our road,
safely housed from an easterly gale
could kill this child's March day, decided,
I called the man dead straight on the phone
and found him home. He's old Pére, our Canon.

I'd never had to ask this question
in my wild life before and phrases
faltered in their indirection.
With priestly patience, punctual silences
he listened as I got it half out
and got the gist I was on about.

'My wife and I've already talked
this matter over and we felt
sure that this was what we liked
given the only alternative. Spelt
out we thought it time to pick
and mark our plot. May we talk?'

'Over the road. The old churchyard.
St. Catherine's in your parish.' He listened.

Then: he wasn't sure what suitable ground
was left in there up on the raised
side. He thought the rest was full
or, under the topsoil, rock and shale.

He must consult his sexton. He'd know
what's available. Then we'd talk.
He'd call me back and tell me how
the lie of the land looked. We'd walk
the churchyard then and choose a spot
that we'd be pleased with as our plot.

Over lunch I told my wife
of my civilised conversation
with the Canon. Too young for grief
as yet, she gayly approved the notion,
served the fish and said, 'Shakespeare
says we're merely passing through nature.'

As nature passes through us, I thought,
then ate up. The Canon phoned.
The safest buy I've ever bought
was on: my plot, my 'piece of land.'
We all agreed to meet at five
outside the gates (if still alive).

The good man sexton showed up too
and knocked three times upon our door.
We four strolled casually those fatal few
yards to the Churchyard faces the shore.

Our dog came too, called Oxymoron.
But he'll be buried in our garden.

The last of winter's sky wept down.
Crows made much crow-talk in their trees.
A pair of pigeons bolted from
a belt of bushes break the leas
and sailed like spirits down the sky
as if they were my wife and me.

The sexton took out measure and hammer
and nail-shaped pegs brought in a bag.
The Canon and I triangled each corner
for the sexton to drive his nails in the sod.
I made some comment on the seepage
from the rise. Or is it drainage?

(Three aging men and a pregnant woman:
father, son and holy ghost,
and mother in the fertile rain
didn't mention the single most
important question of our lives:
whether or not the soul survives.

Christian, Muslim, Buddhist, Jew
all believe in a life hereafter.
I believe all four give true
example for the lie we suffer.
The indomitable truth is death.
After that we belong to the State.

Some live remembered; most pass forgotten
into the inhuman process of Time
unless resurrected from the flotsam and jetsam
for Church and State or their combine.
I don't believe we live again
in some eternal love or pain.)

Done, we removed ourselves away.
The Canon smiled. He'd send the bill.
I wondered where I'd find two grey
lumps of limestone that I'd chisel
our names and dates on myself,
while I have time, in rough relief.

I slipped the sexton his few notes
for his day's trouble; invited himself
and the Canon too for a couple of tots
of whiskey at the house. A cough,
and the Canon said they must get on
to a wedding arrangement down the town.

We thanked them both and shook their hands
and waved goodbye as they drove off.
Back home we poured two personal drams
to toast and clinch our life and love.
Of all the gifts one gives one's woman
none's more binding than a common

plot to lie in all eternity.
You're wedded then as ever you'd be

before the King, the Holy See,
the neighbours and the whole country.
This plot of ground is all I've owned
for sure, in this my native land.

The lot took hardly half an hour
to fulcrum life and love on death.
What can human souls do more
than plot their final act of faith
in human life and love and death
and leave some life from love, not hate?

Once I'd reconciled genesis and nemesis
I went on writing my progression of verses.

Graveyard

The sky's relentless manic blue,
our scrummaged village white; the sea,
insatiate, gurgitates. After mindless
months ploughing this machine that's to me
back in our mud, I take up my trade
from scratch, eye and hand still jiggy.

The books of men I most admire
stack neat across my table
I cannot see or suffer anyone.
Objection breaks apart from absence.
My eye can't peg perspective.

I've turned my bend.
I face and take
that last stretch forever
up Old Stony Batter
to my Stony Joke.

History

Our nights repeat themselves, repeat
their nightmares. Our mornings too
repeat themselves and their dreams of solutions,
of an end to the drums and darkness of ignorance
and bigotry, of an end to marching over the sacrificed dead.
The pall of loneliness on the ideal, on the broken family,
on towns, communities, whole countries, continents.
The repeated waving of banners of victors and vanquished
and the repeated draping of coffins with national colours;
palaver of politicians, compromises of the churches'
conscience; the uncommitted common outsider;
the dedicated killers, the anonymous murdered at night
or in daylight. Street demonstrations and mass funerals.
Even the boredom of tragic death, wanton public destruction
of life's honest efforts for stable security, repeats itself.

Yet such a war-wracked place as ours has multiplied
through the generations despite the repetition of injustice.

Through repeated copulation, birth and death, repeated
different beliefs in a common creed, this hopelessness
still houses so many repeated believing souls.
They never remember. We never forget. Is there a life
of peace after the expiation of indifferent history?

Tipperary

*Tipperary: from the Irish Tiobraidarann: the fountain of
    perception, or enlightenment, intelligence.*

*It's a long way to Tipperary
it's a long way to go* - and devious.
It's a torture of twists, about-turns,
disillusions, disappointments.
The way to Tipperary appears
perennially dark with only
occasional twilights.

If you decide to go to Tipperary
set out while you're young, plucky;
at that age when you're bright-eyed with visions
of radiant horizons of revelation and
    achievement
and you know nothing of twilights or the dark;
that age when all creation, all life shines clear
as spring sunlight, bright as light-catching gold.

When you set out you must go alone.
There are no maps of the way to Tipperary.
Your only compass is your own heart. Trust that!

Some see their Tipperary clearly from the start;
see it's a long road, full of daily pitfalls;
a labyrinth of curious sidestreets, inviting
guesthouses; giddy with the temptations
of those bogey people's trinket stalls'
hokeypokey - daily thieves of eternal energy -

easy come, easy go, you've sold your soul,
you've no more choice. They sell bedlam!

Explore all those sidestreets
enjoy your chosen resthouses
fool with a few trinkets to learn
something of the way to Tipperary.

The long way to Tipperary's darkened
with the shadows of all those
who never got there anyway;
those who settled for some resthouse,
some casual trinket thief of time.
Don't let those shadows,
mumbling in their own gloom,
deter or deviate you.
Hold to your main road. Keep going!

Once you've decided to go to Tipperary
you'll realize you no longer belong to yourself
but must keep Tipperary in your sights daily -
although you can't see it. Purpose is all.
Without your Tipperary you too are a mere
   shadow
at those Limerick Junctions of daily resolution.

On the way to Tipperary keep your eye open
for signals of direction, encouragement:

that nod of understanding, comradeship,
a cherishing arm on your pillow. You'll see
beautiful sights on the way to Tipperary:
man's mirage tales, imagination's monuments.
You'll behold the endless vistas, panoramas
of vision. Be curious about them all
for the gracious gifts they will afford you.
Without them you'd live that much the poorer.

It's a long way to Tipperary
and when you get there
nothing awaits you. You'll find no roadsign,
no brassband and welcoming committee
with a banner proclaiming you're in Tipperary
and a medallion to hang around your neck.
You'll find only what you brought with you
in your heart.

Then, what you must do
is make and leave some record
of what your Tipperary means to you -
as witness for all those behind you
on their ways to their own Tipperaries.

It's a long way to Tipperary
but all our heart lie there.

Also by Desmond O'Grady

Alternative Manners, versions from the Greek of C.P. Cavafy, Salmon Publishing, Galway, 1992.
Ten Modern Arab Poets, versions from the Arabic, Dedalus Press, Dublin, 1992.
The Seven Arab Odes, versions from the Arabic, Agenda Editions/Raven Arts, London-Dublin, 1990.
Alexandria Notebook, poems, Raven Arts, Dublin, 1989.
Grecian Glances, versions from the Greek Anthology, Inkling Press, Cambridge, Mass., 1981.
His Skaldcrane's Nest, poems, Gallery Press, Dublin, 1979.
The Headgear of the Tribe, new and selected poems, Gallery Press, 1979.
A Limerick Rake, versions from the Irish, Gallery Press, 1978.
The Gododdin, versions from the Welsh (with illustrations by Louis le Brocquy), Dolmen Press, Dublin, 1977.
Sing Me Creation, poems, Gallery Press, 1977.
Stations, poems, (with illustrations by Margo Veillon), American University in Cairo Press, 1976.
Separations, poems, Goldsmith Press, Dublin, 1973.
Hellas, a poem, New Writers' Press, Dublin, 1971.
Off Licence, versions from Irish, Armenian, Italian, Dolmen Press, Dublin, 1968.
The Dark Edge of Europe, poems, MacGibbon and Kee, London, 1967.
The Dying Gaul, poems, MacGibbon and Kee, 1967.
Separazioni, poems (with Italian translations), Edizioni Europei, Rome, 1965.
Professor Kelleher and the Charles River, a poem, Carthage Press, Cambridge, Mass., 1964.
Reilly, poems, Phoenix Press, London, 1961.
Chords and Orchestrations, poems, Echo Press, Limerick, 1956.